SCOTT SANDERS   CAROL FINEMAN
UNIBAIL-RODAMCO-WESTFIELD   COLUMBIA LIVE STAGE   SALLY HORCHOW   JAMES L. NEDERLANDER
BENJAMIN LOWY   CINDY AND JAY GUTTERMAN / MARLENE AND GARY COHEN   JUDITH ANN ABRAMS PRODUCTIONS   ROBERT GREENBLATT
STEPHANIE P. McCLELLAND   CANDY SPELLING   JAM THEATRICALS   ROY FURMAN   MICHAEL HARRISON / DAVID IAN
JAMIE DeROY / CATHERINE ADLER / WENDY FEDERMAN / HENI KOENIGSBERG
JAA PRODUCTIONS / STELLA LaRUE / SILVA THEATRICAL GROUP
TOHO CO LTD   JONATHAN LITTMAN   PETER MAY   JANET AND MARVIN ROSEN   SERIFF PRODUCTIONS
IRIS SMITH   BOB BOYETT   THOMAS L. MILLER   LARRY J. KROLL / DOUGLAS L. MEYER   VICTORIA LANG / SCOTT MAURO
BRUNISH / CAIOLA / FULD JR. / EPIC THEATRICALS   TED LIEBOWITZ / LASSEN BLUME BALDWIN
THE JOHN GORE ORGANIZATION   RONALD FRANKEL   CHAR-PARK PRODUCTIONS   CHRIS AND ASHLEE CLARKE
FAKSTON PRODUCTIONS   THE WOODLAND HILLS BROADWAY GROUP
2JS AND AN A. INC.   TOM McGRATH / 42ND.CLUB   DREW HODGES AND PETER KUKIELSKI
JIM FANTACI   FREDERIKE AND BILL HECHT   BRAD LAMM
INDEPENDENT PRESENTERS NETWORK

present

Tootsie

Music and Lyrics by
DAVID YAZBEK

Book by
ROBERT HORN

Based on the story by DON McGUIRE and LARRY GELBART
and the COLUMBIA PICTURES motion picture produced
by PUNCH PRODUCTIONS and starring DUSTIN HOFFMAN

Starring
SANTINO FONTANA

LILLI COOPER   **SARAH STILES**

ANDY GROTELUESCHEN   **MICHAEL McGRATH**   **JOHN BEHLMANN**

with

REG ROGERS and **JULIE HALSTON**

SISSY BELL   BARRY BUSBY   PAULA LEGGETT CHASE   BRITNEY COLEMAN
LESLIE DONNA FLESNER   JENIFER FOOTE   JOHN ARTHUR GREENE   DREW KING
JEFF KREADY   HARRIS MILGRIM   ADAM MONLEY   SHINA ANN MORRIS   JAMES MOYE
KATERINA PAPACOSTAS   NICK SPANGLER   DIANA VADEN   ANTHONY WAYNE

Scenic Design	Costume Design	Lighting Design	Sound Design
DAVID ROCKWELL	**WILLIAM IVEY LONG**	**DONALD HOLDER**	**BRIAN RONAN**

Hair & Wig Design	Make-Up Design	Casting	Music Supervisors
PAUL HUNTLEY	**ANGELINA AVALLONE**	**JIM CARNAHAN, CSA**	**ANDREA GRODY & DEAN SHARENOW**

Vocal and Incidental Arrangements	Dance Arrangements	Orchestrations	Music Coordinator
ANDREA GRODY	**DAVID CHASE**	**SIMON HALE**	**DEAN SHARENOW**

Production Management	Production Stage Manager	Associate Director	Associate Choreographer
AURORA PRODUCTIONS	**SCOTT TAYLOR ROLLISON**	**DAVE SOLOMON**	**BARRY BUSBY**

Marketing Supervision	Advertising & Marketing	Press Representation	General Management
MICHELE GRONER	**SPOTCO**	**POLK & CO.**	**BESPOKE THEATRICALS**

Music Director
ANDREA GRODY

Choreographed by
DENIS JONES

Directed by
SCOTT ELLIS

Original Cast Album Available on Decca Broadway
The producers wish to express their appreciation to the Theatre Development Fund for its support of this production.

ISBN 978-1-5400-6114-0

Visit Hal Leonard Online at
www.halleonard.com

Contact us:
Hal Leonard
7777 West Bluemound Road
Milwaukee, WI 53213
Email: info@halleonard.com

In Europe, contact:
Hal Leonard Europe Limited
42 Wigmore Street
Marylebone, London, W1U 2RN
Email: info@halleonardeurope.com

In Australia, contact:
Hal Leonard Australia Pty. Ltd.
4 Lentara Court
Cheltenham, Victoria, 3192 Australia
Email: info@halleonard.com.au

OPENING NUMBER

Words and Music by
DAVID YAZBEK

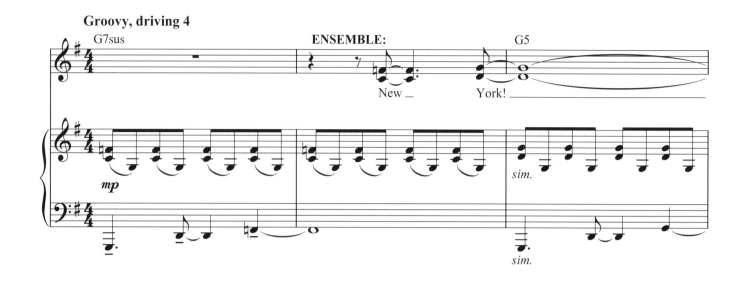

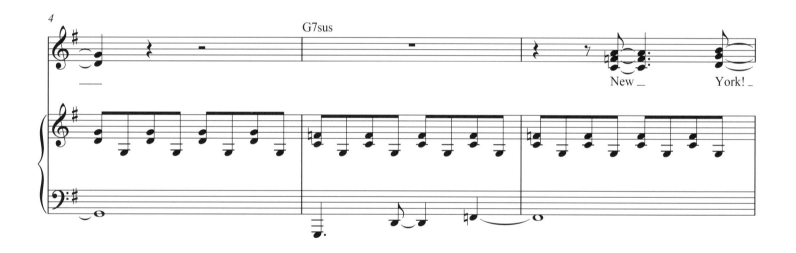

Any dream can be a dream come true in... New _ York! _   **MICHAEL:** *Underneath this city that's all*

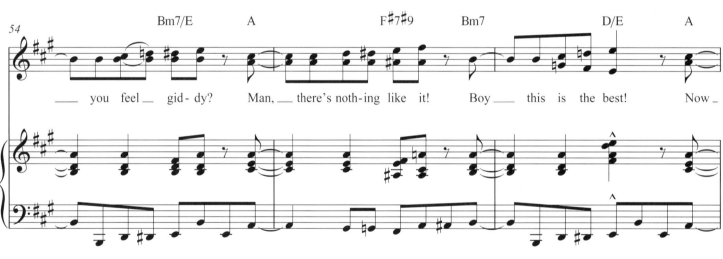

pavement is a city that's all heart.   **ENSEMBLE:** God _____ this is ex - cit - ing. Don't _

_ you feel _ gid - dy? Man, _ there's noth - ing like it! Boy _ this is the best! Now _

_ your light is blaz - ing! Wow, _ this is a cit - y! Is - n't this a - maz - ing? Are -

That does-n't mean he is-n't real good. _ No one in town would dis-a-gree.

He real-ly could be good as Giel - gud, _ but you won't see his name on

the mar - quee. And now there's some-thing quite fa-

mil - iar, _ he feels it ris-ing like the moon.

WHADDYA DO

Words and Music by
DAVID YAZBEK

Bright, rolling tempo

Whad-d-ya do when sud-den-ly you re-al-ize the cal-en-dar in-

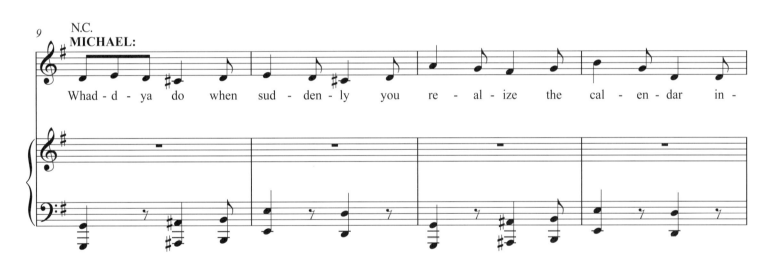

side your head is run-ning out of pag-es? Whad-d-ya do if

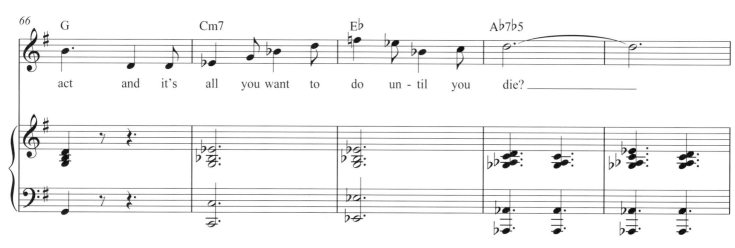

WHAT'S GONNA HAPPEN

Words and Music by
DAVID YAZBEK

Fast Latin, in 2

SANDY:

I know what's gon-na hap-pen. I'll try to go to bed with fear of fail-ure

flap-pin' like a fruit bat in my head, I'll sleep for half an ho-ur, the clock-'ll ring at

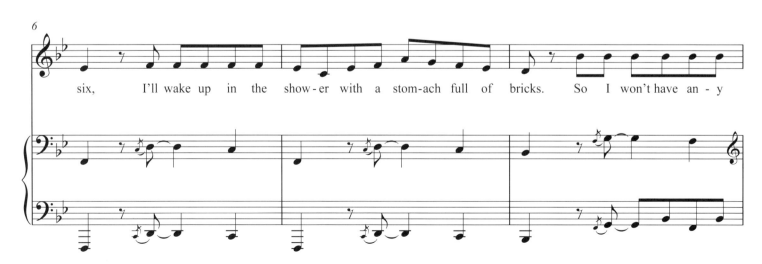

six, I'll wake up in the show-er with a stom-ach full of bricks. So I won't have an-y

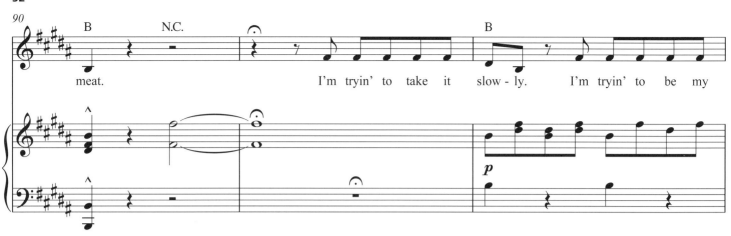

meat.   I'm tryin' to take it slow-ly.   I'm tryin' to be my

best.   I'm tryin' to be more ho-ly, less bit-ter and de-pressed.   I'm read-ing Eck-hart

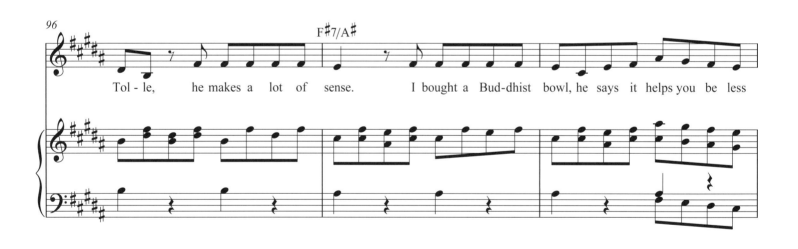

Tol-le,   he makes a lot of sense.   I bought a Bud-dhist bowl, he says it helps you be less

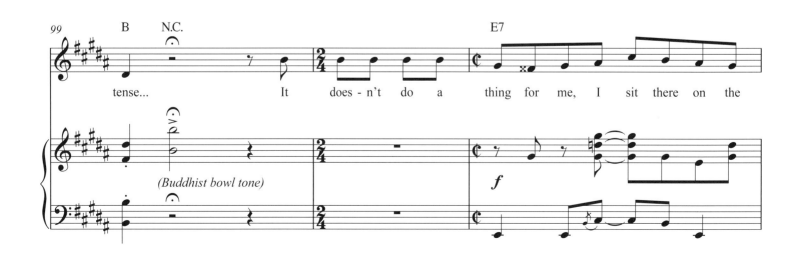

tense...   It does-n't do a thing for me, I sit there on the

(Buddhist bowl tone)

when it's time to pack your bags and say, "That's it!" You

know what's gon - na hap - pen? I know what's gon - na hap - pen!

Here's what's gon - na hap - pen: I quit. I

quit. I quiii _____ t!

I WON'T LET YOU DOWN

Words and Music by
DAVID YAZBEK

Moderate Ballad, con moto

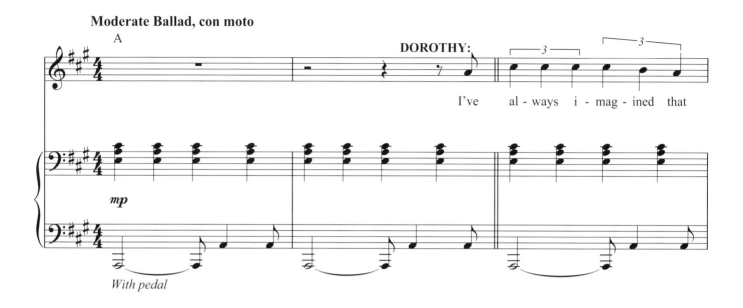

DOROTHY:
I've al - ways i - mag - ined that

you are the flow - er and I am the dirt. My

world spins a - round you, when - ev - er you fall, I'm the one who gets hurt.

I'M ALIVE

Words and Music by
DAVID YAZBEK

Bright 60s Rock

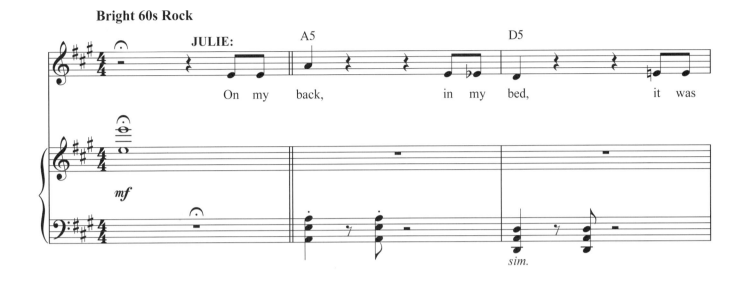

On my back, in my bed, it was

dark, I was dead. (gasp!) Could-n't move, could-n't walk, could-n't

breathe and I sure ___ could-n't talk. No more dusk, no more

46

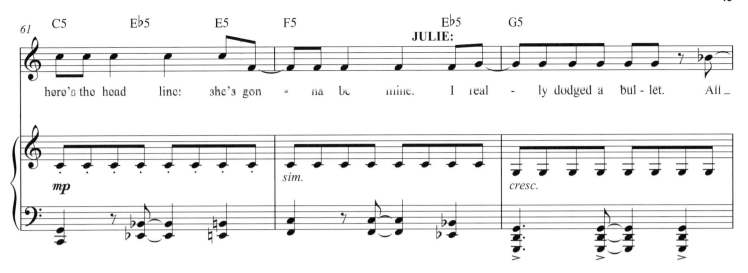

here's the head- line: she's gon - na be mine. I real - ly dodged a bul - let. All _

_ the plumb-ing's work- ing. Thank _ God they did - n't bur - y me, 'cause

I'm _____ a - live! _____

WOMEN:
A - live, _ a - live, _ a - live, _ a - live, _

MEN:

THERE WAS JOHN

Words and Music by
DAVID YAZBEK

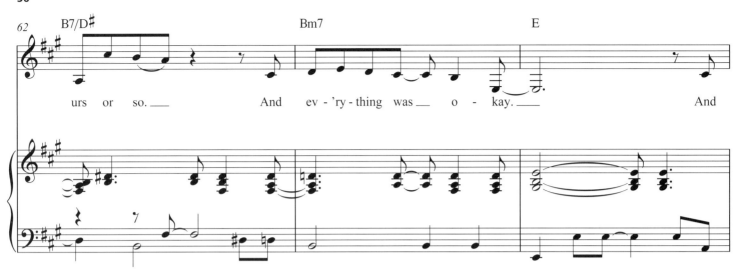

urs or so. ___ And ev-'ry-thing was ___ o - kay. ___ And

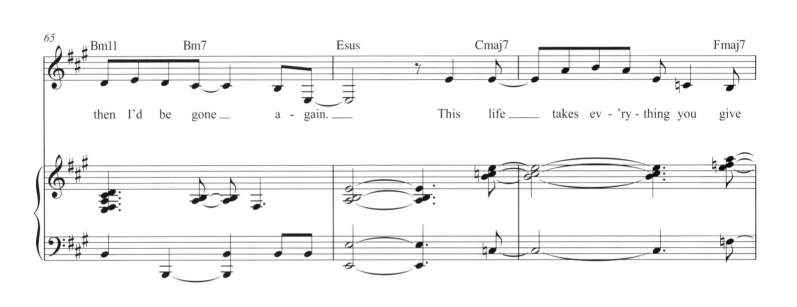

then I'd be gone ___ a - gain. ___ This life ___ takes ev-'ry-thing you give

it, like a pup-py or a kid. ___ **JULIE:** But, if ___ you real-ly love it, you

I LIKE WHAT SHE'S DOING

Words and Music by
DAVID YAZBEK

Poco meno mosso e molto Siciliano

Poco meno mosso e molto "Ricky Ricardo plays Studio 54"

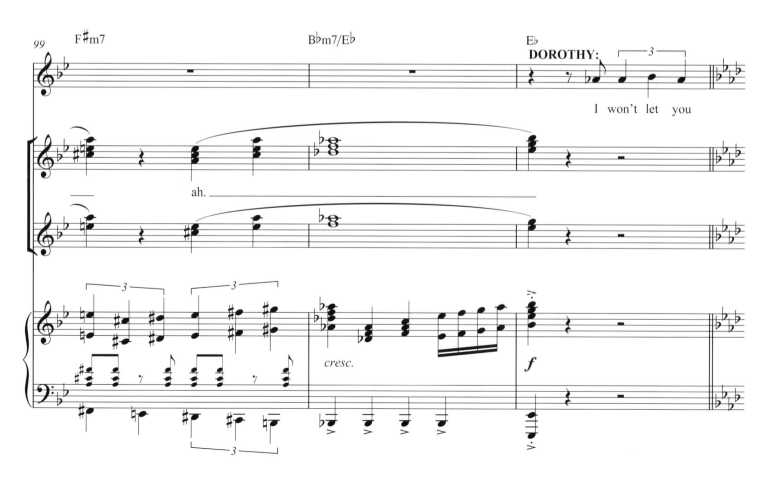

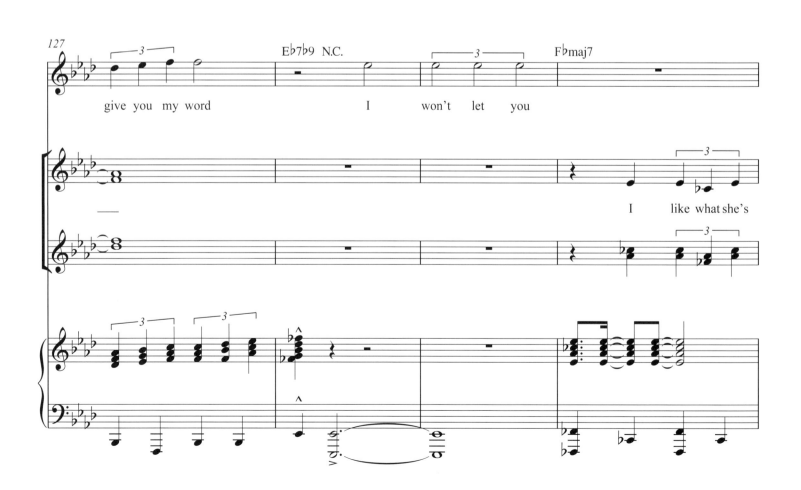

WHO ARE YOU?

Words and Music by
DAVID YAZBEK

Moderate Ballad, molto rubato

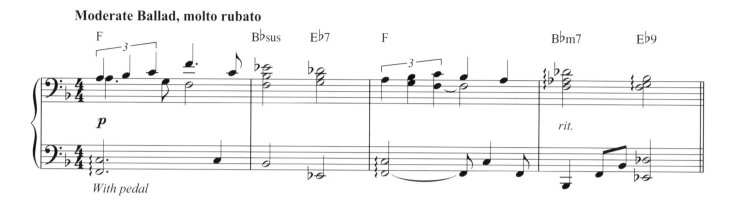

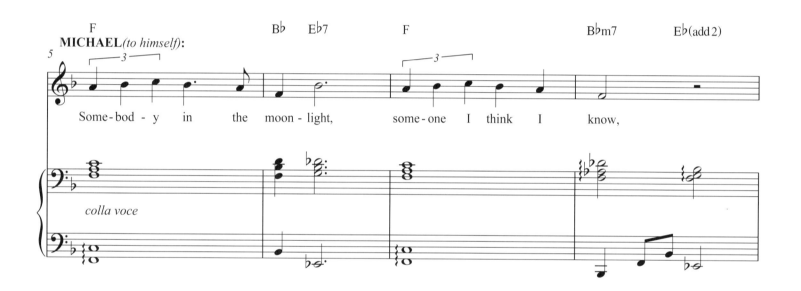

MICHAEL *(to himself):*

Some-bod-y in the moon-light, some-one I think I know,

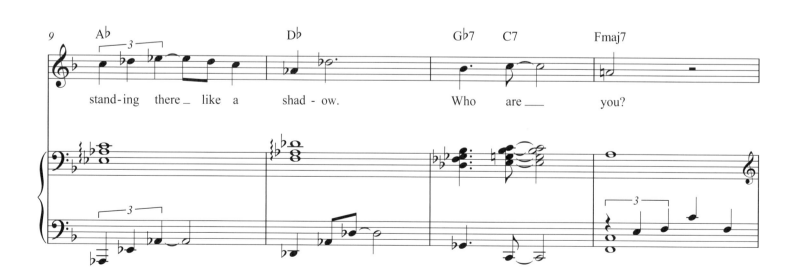

stand-ing there __ like a shad-ow. Who are __ you?

UNSTOPPABLE

Words and Music by
DAVID YAZBEK

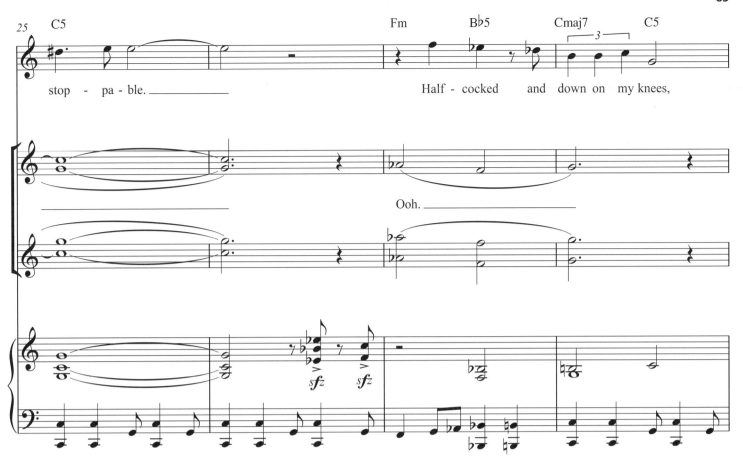

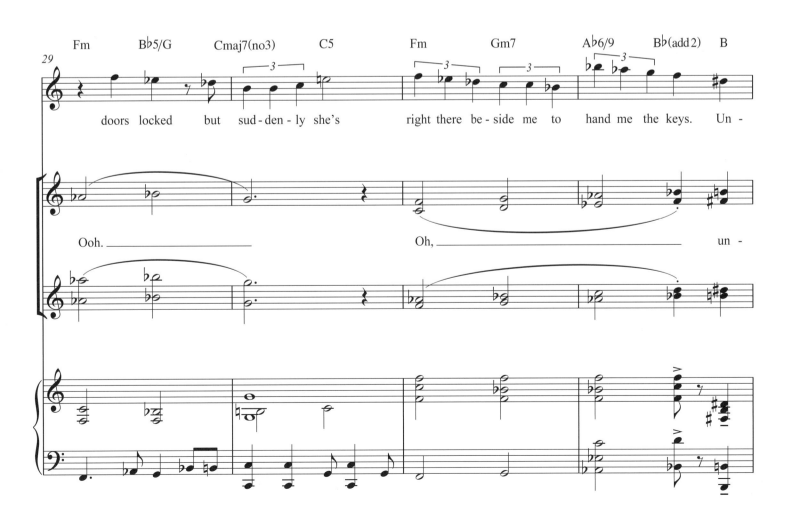

stop - pa - ble. _____ Un - stop - pa - ble. _____

stop - pa - ble. _____

We got the role!   We got the gig!   We got con - trol!

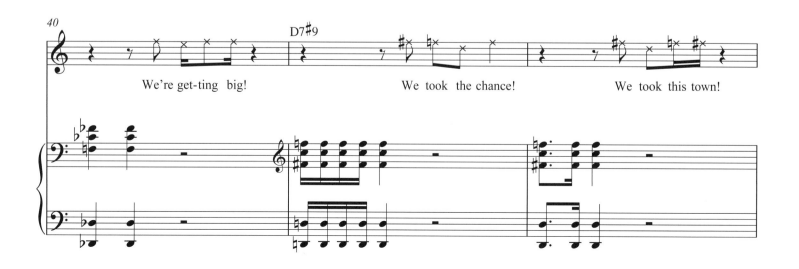

We're get-ting big!   We took the chance!   We took this town!

Told you be-fore, show me the door, I'll kick it down!   When I put on the

WOMEN:
Oh! _____

MEN:

wig and the dress I'm un-flap-pa-ble. _____   You can't start to chart

Bow bow ba bow ba bow bow ba bow ba bow.

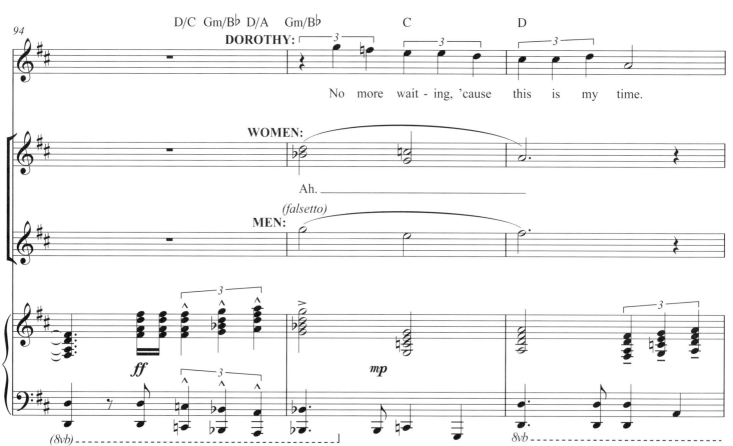

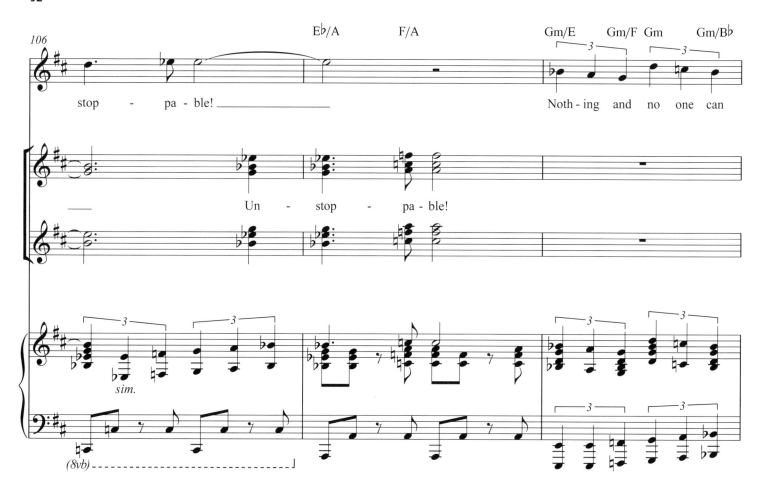

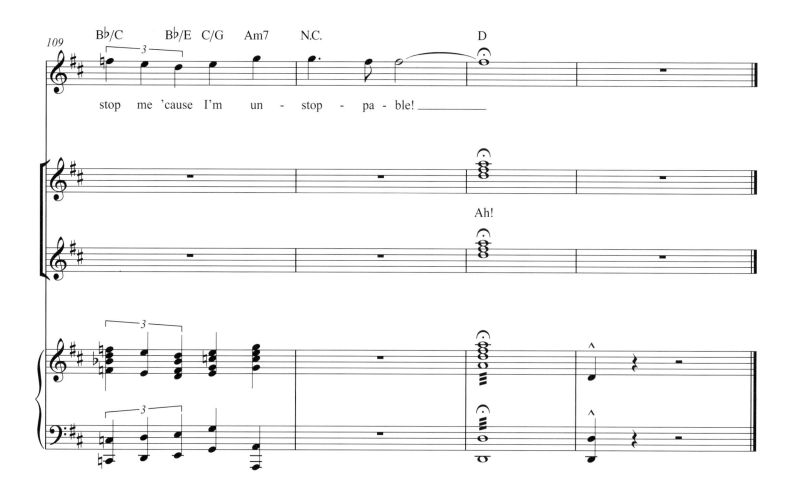

JEFF SUMS IT UP

Words and Music by
DAVID YAZBEK

Deliberately

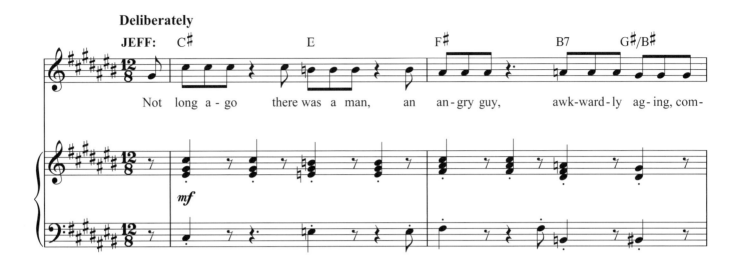

JEFF: Not long a-go there was a man, an an-gry guy, awk-ward-ly ag-ing, com-

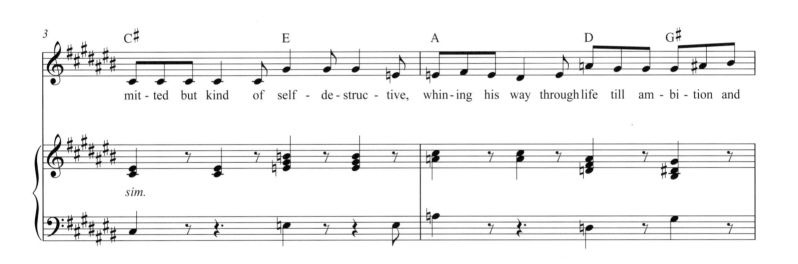

mit-ted but kind of self-de-struc-tive, whin-ing his way through life till am-bi-tion and

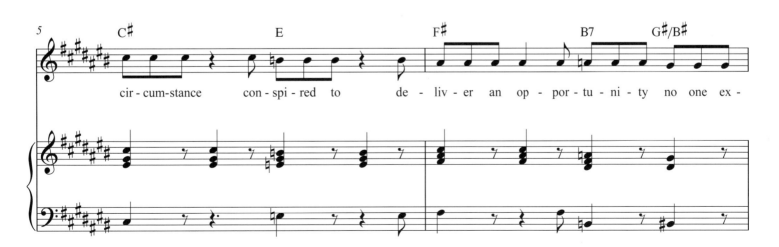

cir-cum-stance con-spi-red to de-liv-er an op-por-tu-ni-ty no one ex-

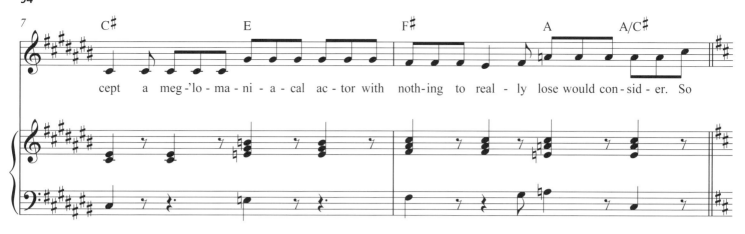

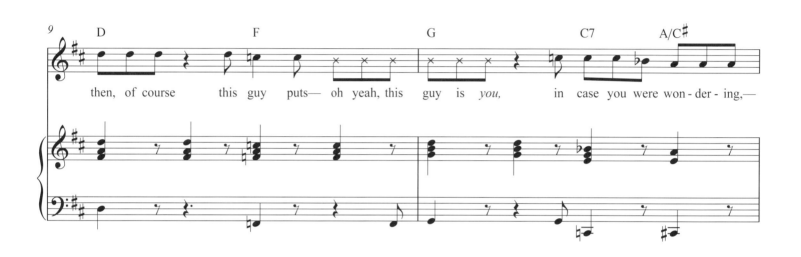

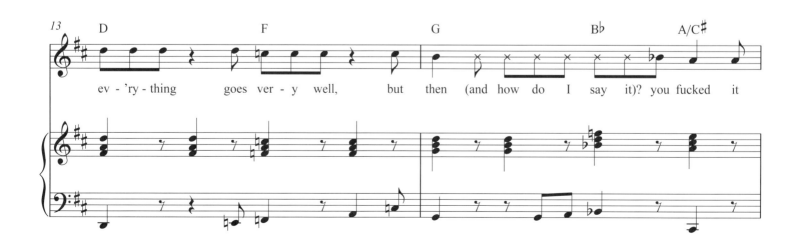

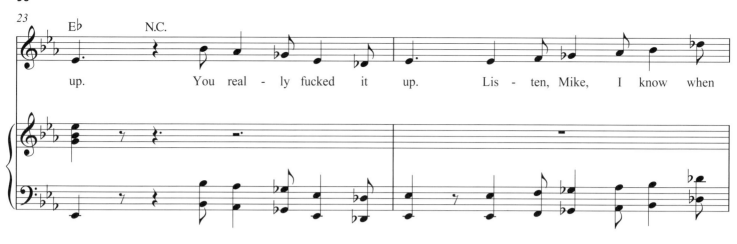

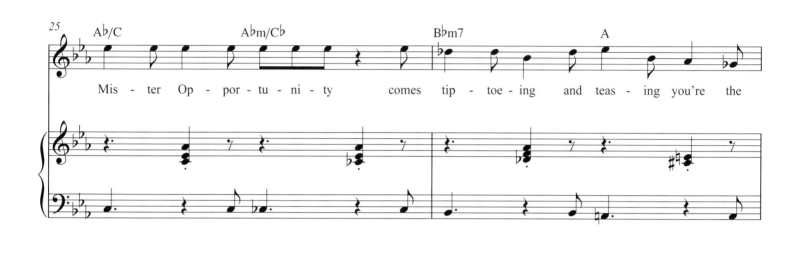

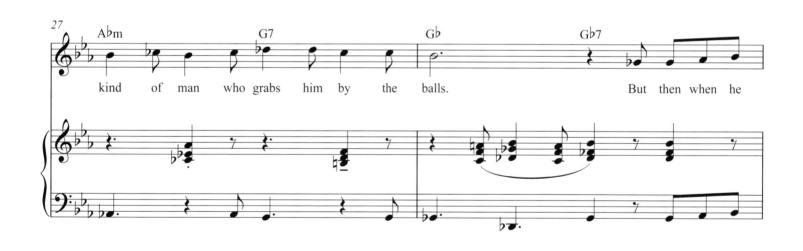

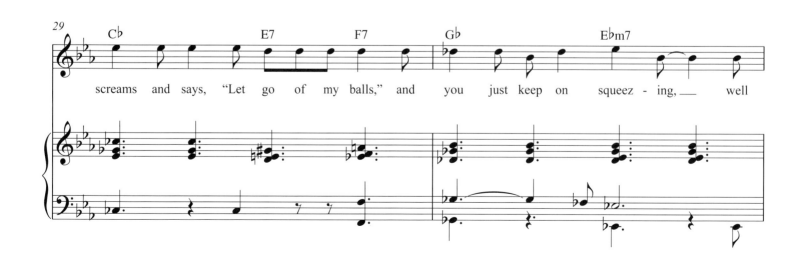

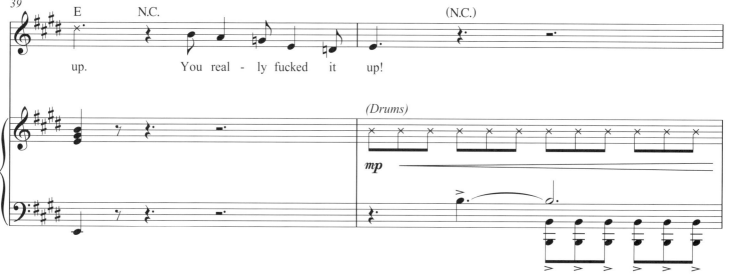

up. You real - ly fucked it up!

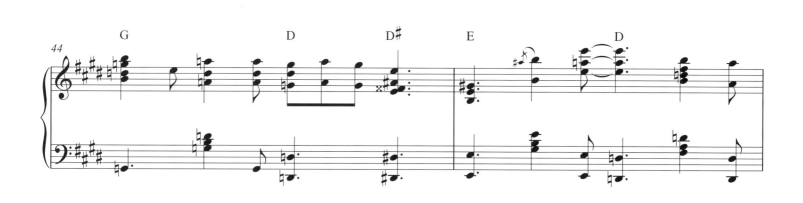

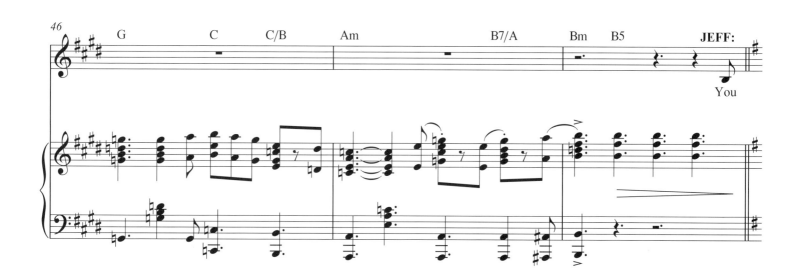

JEFF:

You

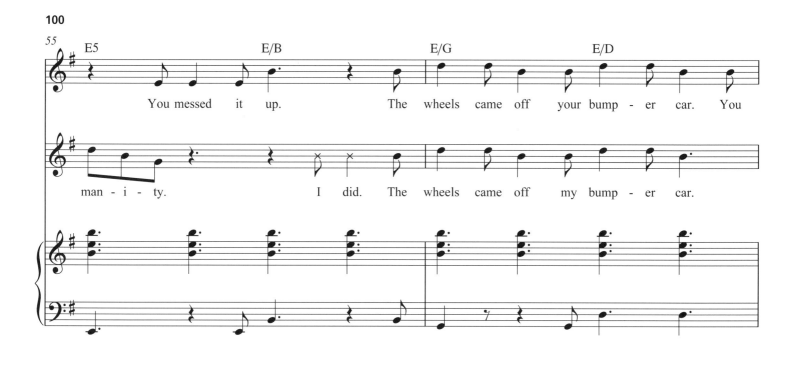

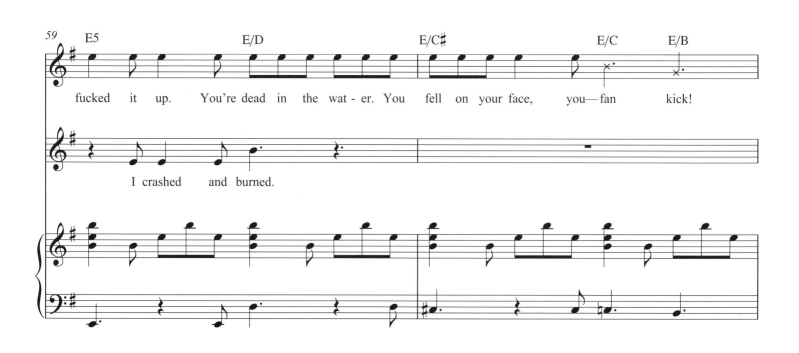

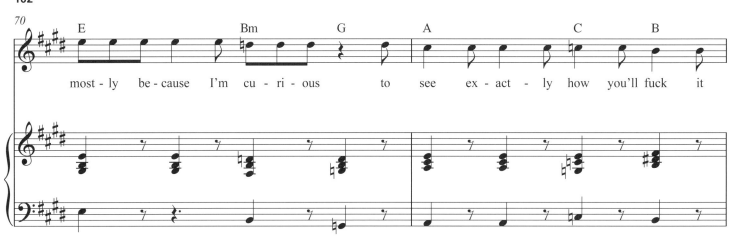

mostly because I'm curious to see exactly how you'll fuck it

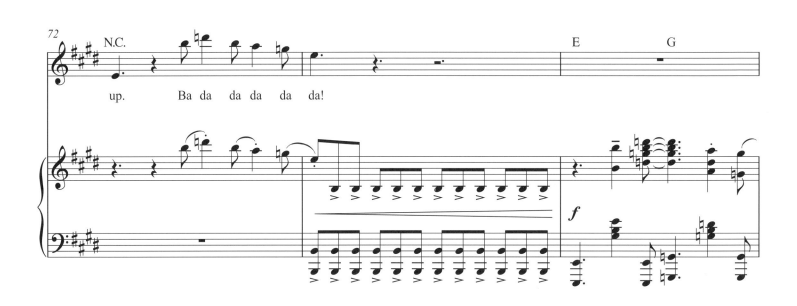

up. Ba da da da da da!

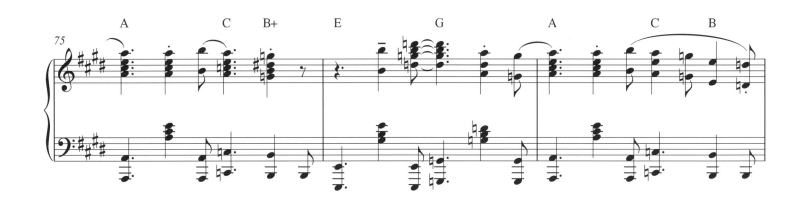

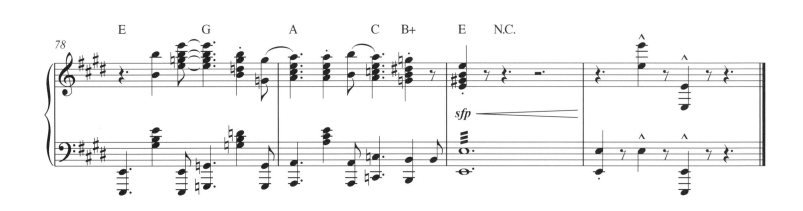

GONE, GONE GONE

Words and Music by
DAVID YAZBEK

JULIE:
I woke __ up this morn-ing __ out - ta my brain. An un - fa - mil - iar feel - ing __ like __ I'm gon - na go in - sane. Scream - ing like a

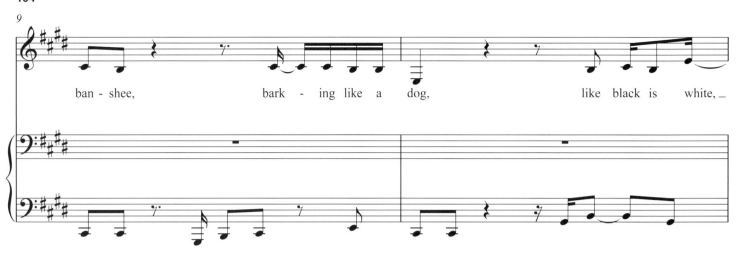

ban - shee,   bark - ing like a dog,   like black is white, __

__ like day is night, __ like I'm walk - ing in a to - tal fog. __ And I'm

3 WOMEN:

And I'm

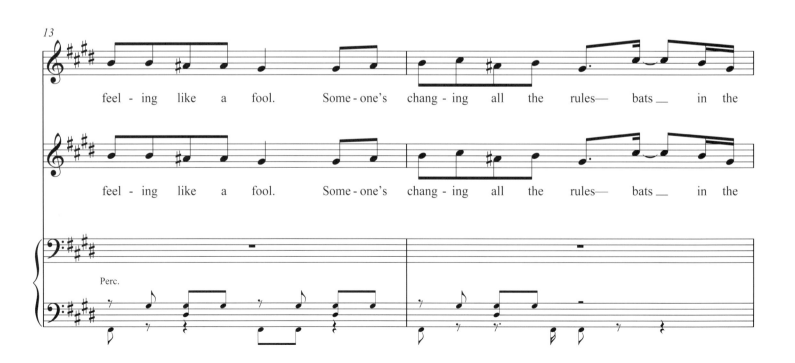

feel - ing like a fool.   Some - one's chang - ing all the rules— bats __ in the

feel - ing like a fool.   Some - one's chang - ing all the rules— bats __ in the

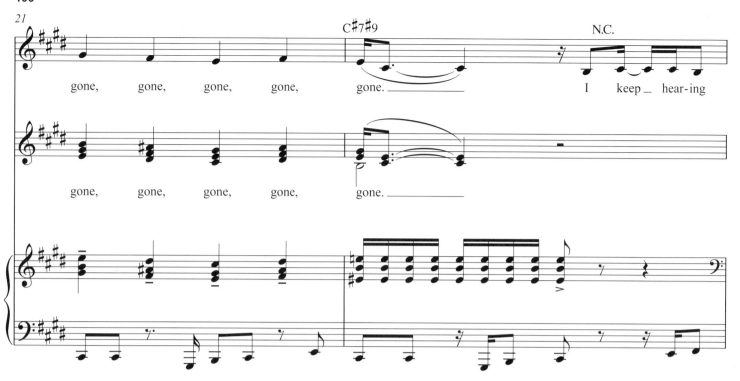

do mon and I can't make it stop. My mind is bruised, __

__ I'm so con-fused, __ wait-ing for the oth-er __ shoe to drop.

3 WOMEN:

And it's

all be-cause of you, 'cause you're chang-ing all the rules. Bats __ in the

Bats __ in the

gone, gone, gone, gone, gone. _____ I'm a

gone, gone, gone, gone, gone. _____

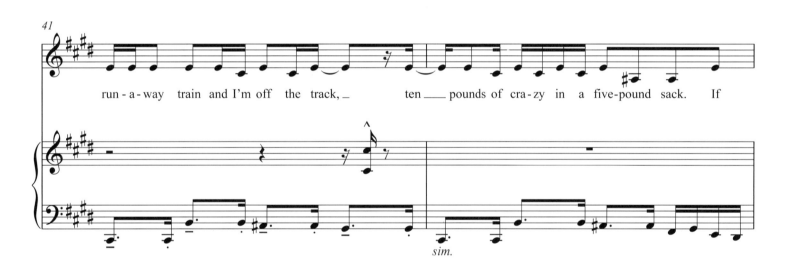

run-a-way train and I'm off the track, _ ten ___ pounds of cra-zy in a five-pound sack. If

sim.

six were nine, _ that's how I feel. _ Three _ fries short _ of a Hap-py Meal. _ I'm

3 WOMEN:

I'm

THIS THING

Words and Music by
DAVID YAZBEK

Grandiose

MAX VAN HORN:
What is this thing I'm feel - ing,

fp

With pedal

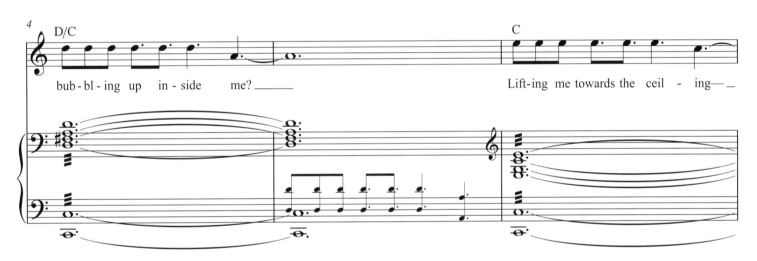

bub - bl - ing up in - side me? _____

Lift - ing me towards the ceil - ing—

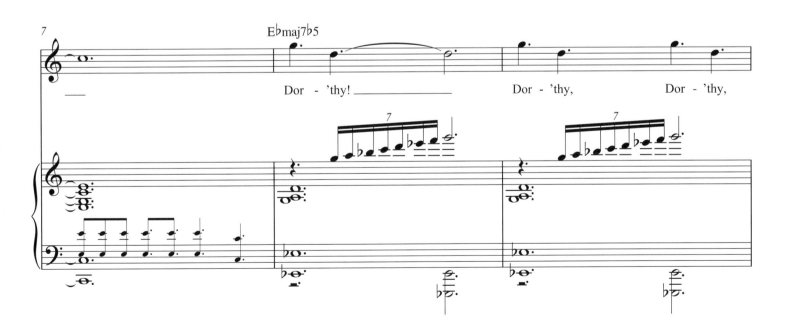

Dor - 'thy! _____

Dor - 'thy, Dor - 'thy,

right for the fe - male ___ moth. That moth is you! What can I do? What is this thing that I'm feel - ing? It's odd, you're so old, I'm so young and my abs are like slabs of fine gran - ite. My bod is like gold and I'm hung and you're old, oh I said that, but

THE MOST IMPORTANT NIGHT OF MY LIFE

Words and Music by
DAVID YAZBEK

Just don't pan - ic, don't get man - ic, re - lax - a - tion is key! This is the...

WOMEN:
The most im - por - tant night, the most im -

RON & MEN:
The most im - por - tant night, the most im -

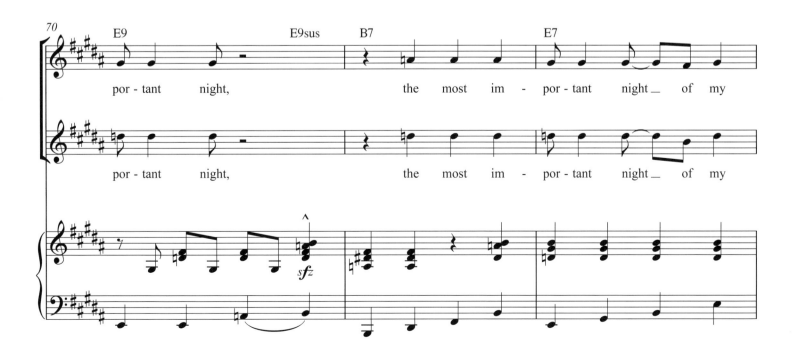

por - tant night, the most im - por - tant night___ of my

por - tant night, the most im - por - tant night___ of my

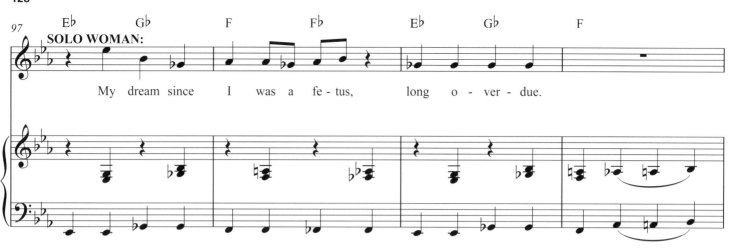

My dream since I was a fe-tus, long o-ver-due.

Ev-'ry sin-gle liv-ing hu-man be-ing's got to a-gree.

Ev-'ry sin-gle liv-ing hu-man be-ing's got to a-gree. This is the...

The most im-por-tant night, the most im-por-tant night,

The most im - por - tant night___ of my...

The most im - por - tant night___ of my...

The most im - por - tant night___ of my...

the most im - por - tant night___ of my...

RITA. *Half hour, everyone.*

Very broadly

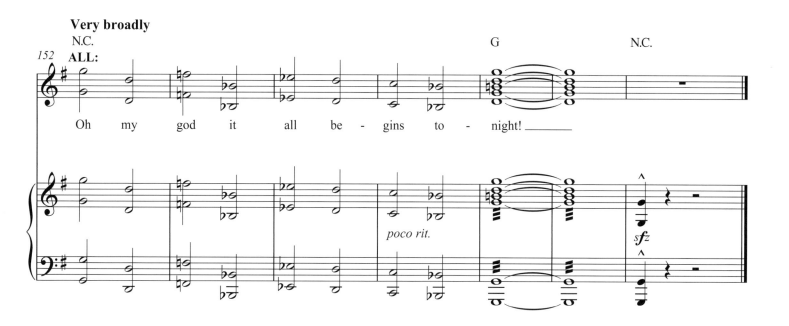

ALL:

Oh my god it all be - gins to - night! _____

poco rit.

sfz

TALK TO ME DOROTHY

Words and Music by
DAVID YAZBEK

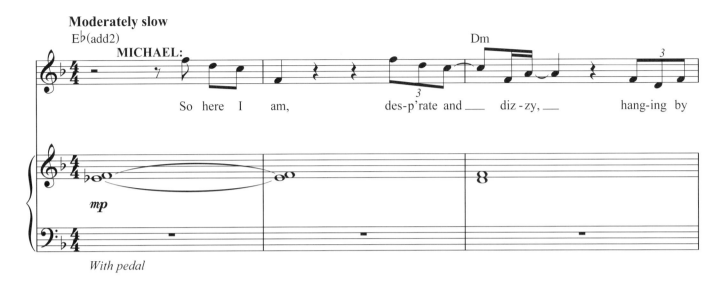

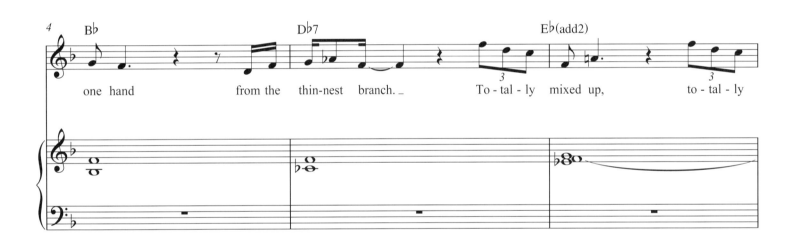

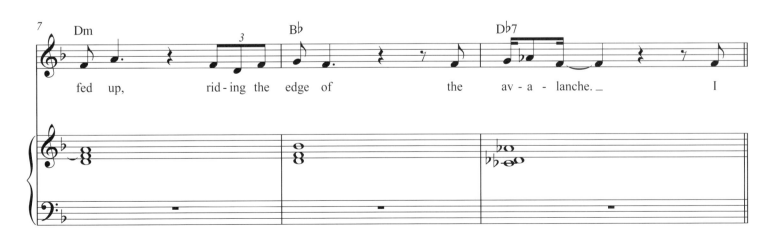

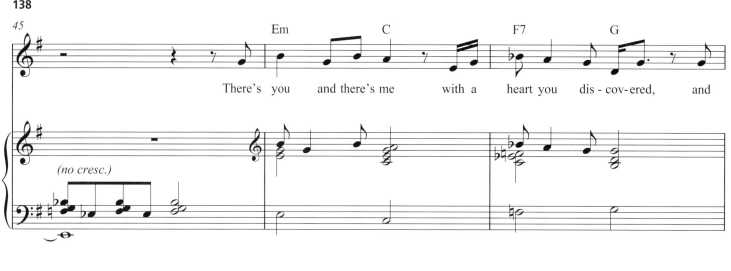

There's you and there's me with a heart you dis-cov-ered, and

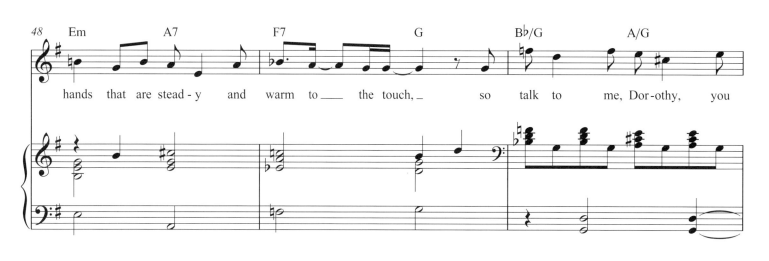

hands that are stead-y and warm to ___ the touch, _ so talk to me, Dor-othy, you

taught me how to sing. Can you help me, Dor-othy? I need you so

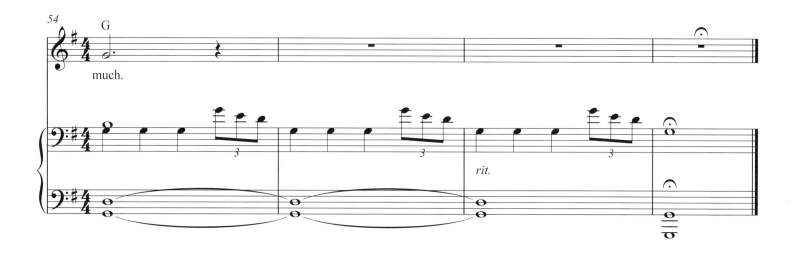

much.

ARRIVEDERCI!

Words and Music by
DAVID YAZBEK

MICHAEL'S REPRISE

Words and Music by
DAVID YAZBEK

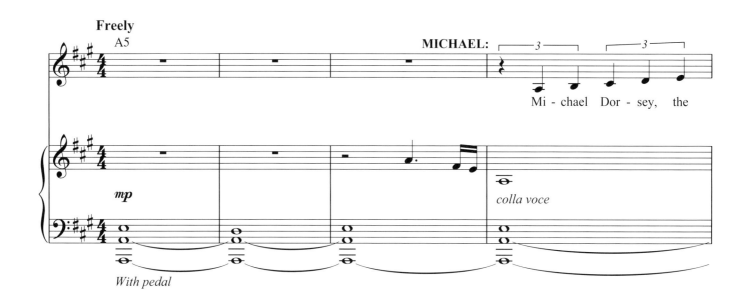

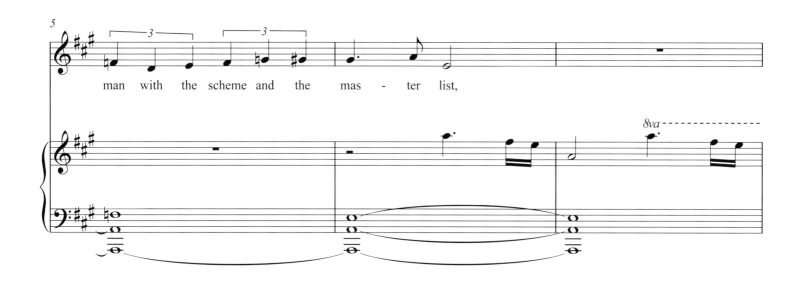

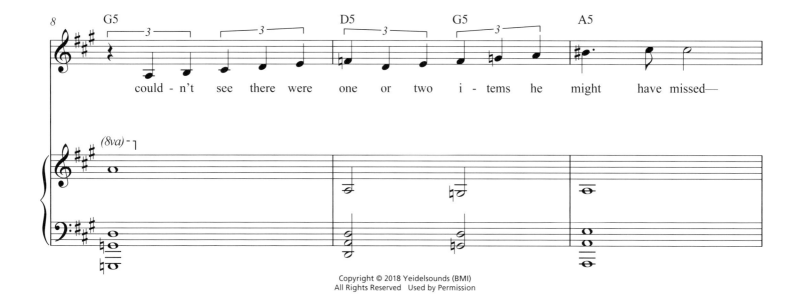